Love has a Name... JESUS

MIGDALIA CENTENO
Author

Dedication

I want to dedicate this book to my parents,
Roberto and Iris M. Rivera,
who are with the Lord Jesus Christ in Heaven.
I miss and love you so much.

Contents

What people are saying about
Love has a Name…JESUS!

"Live life to share, share life to exist." Migdalia Centeno, my mom, shares her intimate and transformational moments from her life which are very relatable in one way or another. She has been a role model in my life and to many others. "Love has a Name...Jesus" will be a blessing, and her personal story will impact lives." **Millicent Centeno**

"She lets readers in and allows them to get a glimpse of what her life was like before she had a life-changing encounter with Jesus Christ. Every woman, in some way, can relate to her story. Her testimony gives hope and reminds us all that Jesus indeed came to save the brokenhearted." **Irene M. Mon**

"I have known Migdalia for over 30 years, and I must say that as I read the chapters in her book it just took me back to realize how much God truly has made Himself so real in her life. As you read how God can transform with the power of His Love, Grace, and Hope, you will desire, if you haven't yet, to receive and encounter the same spiritual experiences. Be ready to open your heart as you will supernaturally encounter God's amazing grace." **Maria C. Rodriguez**

"I am able to express with great pleasure that it is wonderful to witness the great works that God can do in the life of a person. The author sets the way for answers to frequent questions that you may have as a reader about God's love, transformation, redemption and loving kindness. It is imperative to understand that God once again has done what He knows how to do best......He has loved His creation with everlasting love and has revealed Himself through such powerful and personal experiences as you will find in this book. My prayer is that you will also encounter God's treasures for your life through a personal encounter with His Love through, "Love has a Name...Jesus." **Rosa I. Vera**

"Look what the Lord has done and how He was able to transform an unpolished stone and convert it into a Diamond of Love." **Alicia Ramirez**

"Religion versus relationship; this book reveals how Jesus came to connect us to God the Father and to establish a relationship with creation, it allows readers from all walks of life to see that Jesus is all about relationship and not about religion."

Debbie Rivera

Love has a Name…JESUS

Acknowledgments

First and foremost, I want to give all the glory and honor to my Lord Jesus Christ for loving me with unconditional love. I am blessed to have had such beautiful encounters in Your presence that have transformed my life.

I would like to thank my husband, Domiason, for taking this journey along with me, called marriage. You have always encouraged me to reach new heights, and you have demonstrated your support whenever I wanted to give up. I would not have been here had it not been for all your prayers and your love. I will forever love you!

Millicent and Dommasin, I want to say that I am the most blessed mother; I thank God for choosing me to be your mom. I am so proud of the woman and man you have become in the Lord. Thank you for the support and encouragement that both of you have given me.

I want to thank every person that contributed through their gifting by proofreading, editing and praying for me through this process. Your generous time has not gone unnoticed, and I will forever be grateful for sowing into this project, **Love has a Name…Jesus.**

Introduction

"Every moment is a fresh beginning."
T.S. Eliot

Introduction

My desire is as people read the pages of **Love has a Name…Jesus** that it will create a hunger, thirst and desire to have a supernatural and personal experience with Jesus Christ. Every chapter describes the different experiences I've had with the Holy Spirit who made Jesus a reality in my life.

During the course of one year, I encountered His presence in a remarkable way that marked my life forever. The experiences began with a series of moments of healing and deliverance. For 11 years, I had a hardened heart because of bitterness, resentment and anger that were due to many disappointments. I felt abandoned and rejected while being amongst the crowd.

As a result of my hardened heart, I became desperate to seek God. In my walk with God, I gained healing, deliverance and restoration just like the woman in the Bible who had the issue of blood.

In the book of Mark 5:24-34 and the book of Luke 8:42-48, there is a story of a woman who was battling with an issue of blood for 12 years. Her sickness isolated her from her surroundings; as it was declared in the Law of Moses, she was considered unclean due to her illness.

She was rejected for 12 years and had to remain isolated as a form of punishment. She tried everything in her power to find a cure or solution to her problem. Nonetheless, she failed with every attempt.

The scriptures declare that the issue of blood had only grown worse (see Mark 5:26). She was left without any protection and was basically economically stripped without any healing.

One day, she went to the place where she knew Jesus would be. Jesus was in the midst of a great multitude. Although she knew she would be greatly punished for being in public, she gave up her will and continued to seek Him.

Jesus was surrounded by so many people that it was inevitable of him not being touched by the multitude. She said within her, *"If I can only touch the hem of His garment, I will be healed"* (Mark 5:28).

The woman managed to squeeze through the crowd and touched the hem of Jesus' garment. Immediately, Jesus stopped in the midst of the crowd. He then asked, *"…Somebody touched Me, for I perceived power going out from Me"* (Luke 8:46).

She then revealed herself and admitted to touching him. Due to her faith, He pronounced her whole/healed. You may find that you too can relate to the woman with the issue of blood. Perhaps you have tried to do it on your own but the problem has kept getting worse.

It may be that you have been looking in the wrong places for acceptance because of rejection and abandonment.

It may be possible that you have been hurt over and over again due to disappointments. You may have also put your hope in people, places and things but the results have been in vain.

It is my desire that as you read about the works of the Holy Spirit that you may also experience a powerful encounter with Jesus.

Love has a Name…Jesus, has been birthed to inspire and create a desire of that encounter for all who will read about my experiences.

Prayer

Father God, I pray You become a reality in the life of every reader as they begin to explore the Following pages of the book.
Amen!

The Transformation

"Holiness consists of three things – separation from sin, dedication to God, transformation into Christ's image."
James H. Aughey

Chapter One

The word *transform* is an action word. It signifies that something has changed or converted. Let me share my experience about how God transformed my life. His supernatural power transformed me with a simple touch that penetrated deep within my heart. God's divine power began to change me from the inside out.

There was a shine upon my face that had not been there before, and it was evident that God had truly done something in my life. It was an experience unlike anything I had ever encountered. It was the overwhelming power of God's love that had transformed the deepest part of my heart. Jesus' loving touch is supernatural and out of this world. His love can be sensed and seen as an *"Unlimited Power"*.

His touch is so gentle yet strong enough to penetrate and transform even the hardest heart in a moment, in the twinkling of an eye (1 Corinthians 15:52). Jesus' love is powerful enough to bring about a change in our life, especially when we allow the Holy Spirit to have His way.

The Holy Spirit works in collaboration and executes Jesus' Word with His presence, especially in the hearts of the disappointed and abused.

Years of disappointments, abuse, and constant let downs will take a toll on a person's heart. Bitterness and resentment will begin to take root and wrap itself around a person's hurting heart. This was exactly what happened to me.

I spent years seeking and searching for people to affirm and pour pure gestures of love into my life. It seemed impossible.

The kind of love I desired could not be provided by any human being. Song of Solomon 3:4 declares, *"…When I found the one I love. I held him and would not let him go…"* (NKJV).

Throughout time, I learned that only in Jesus could it be found. Being unloved created insecurities and complex issues within myself. As a result, without noticing, I became a people-pleaser.

At an early age, I was taught how to do household chores. When I was 11 years old, my mother decided to return to work after being a housewife for 12 years caring for her children. My parents believed this would prepare me for marriage.

"As a result, without noticing, I became a people- pleaser."

My father was a very hard working man. Many times, he worked two jobs to make sure he was providing for his family. My mom went back to work once my younger sister started school.

I remember my mom telling me to go with her to the kitchen because she was going to teach me how to cook. I recall her telling me,

19

"You have to put this much rice, oil, and water, and make sure you stir the rice so it won't stick to the cooking pot".
She walked me through every step, even how to bring the fire to a simmer so the rice wouldn't burn.

I had to learn how to clean the house the way she expected it to be cleaned. During those years, that is what girls would do to help their mothers. My mother wanted to make sure that she had taught me everything that I needed to know so that I would be ready for marriage.

I wanted to please my parents by obeying, cleaning, and cooking. I wanted and needed their affirmation.
Focus on the Family Singapore wrote an article called the 5 A's for Your Family indicates,

> *"Affirmation is the expression of acceptance. A parent's affirmation gives security, so children who are secure in their parents' love are less likely to seek acceptance from other sources in future. Praise and encouragement give significance, so make positive statements about who they are, their qualities, character and potential."* (2015)

I wanted to hear them express that they appreciated me by helping with the house chores and cooking dinner for the family, but it did not happen. This made me feel like they did not love me.

Of course, later in life, I came to learn that my parents had a rough childhood and their parents were not affectionate. They were only mirroring what they had learned from their parents. My parents did love their children and for them it was demonstrated by providing a roof over our heads and food on the table.

Another norm in the household was that there was no need to pursue a higher education after high school. In our traditional Hispanic culture, women were not encouraged to further their education.

According to Latina women and higher education – making it happen states,

> *"It wasn't too long ago that the primary lifetime expectations for women included getting married and having children. These traditions were — and in many regards continue to be — more entrenched in the Latino community, but things are changing."*

(Horwedel, D.M., 2007)

It was something rare in our family. However, deep down in my heart, I always knew I was destined for something greater, a unique purpose.

By the age of sixteen, when I was in the 10th grade, I got married and had my first child. I thought about quitting school to become a housewife. I was willing to sacrifice my education to take care of my family, which did not seem like a bad idea, until my husband told me that I was not quitting high school. I was going to graduate even though I had my daughter.

"I began to search for something that was beyond my own strength."

Being married and a young mother at the age of 16, added another set of challenges that turned into more disappointments. As the years moved on, the disappointments piled up. I began to be consumed by them. Every moment of the day I thought *"Why me?"*

As I look back, I realize that God was always with me. In my mess, I was still functional. I would go to work, come home, and take care of my family in the midst of being unhappy.

Now I understand that the disappointments catapulted me into desperation.

I began to search for something that was beyond my own strength. I tried for so many years to do it with my own understanding. King Solomon declared in Proverbs 3:5, *"Trust in the Lord with all your heart, and lean not on your own understanding;"* (NKJV).

I thought I was in control, but I was not. I thought I was able to fix my life and my marriage but that was not the case. Even though I was thinking this way, it got worse with each day that passed.

I could not stop the downward spiral in which my life was heading. I tried on my own, over and over, but it was in vain. In the back of my mind, I knew that I had to call out to Jesus.

Jeremiah 33:3 indicates,

> *"Call to Me, and I will answer you, and show you great and mighty things, which you do not know"* (NKJV).

I always knew deep down in my heart that if I called out to Him, He would come to my rescue.

My only struggle was that I did not want to surrender my

will because I was scared to let go of the control. However, I got to a place where I decided I could no longer lie to myself.

I was in a dark place in my life, and the only one that could pull me out of my problems and change my circumstances was Jesus. I cried out to Him, and He came to my rescue. Jesus saved me! He extended His right hand and pulled me out of that dark place.

Matthew 14:30 mentions, "…he cried out, saying, "Lord, save me!" The scripture declares that in one occasion, Jesus was walking upon the waters during a storm.

"Jesus was waiting for me to call out to Him and He came to my rescue."

Peter began to walk upon the waters, but suddenly he began to sink once he allowed his surroundings to dictate his feelings. Human feelings are real and God placed it in His creation to serve a purpose but when channeled in a negative way, it can cause destruction to a person.

However, Peter quickly reflected and called out to the Lord. Jesus extended His hand and pulled him out of the stormy waters. In the same way, my soul was pulled out of the dark place that my surroundings had placed me in.

Jesus was waiting for me to call out to Him so that He could come to my rescue. I recognize that the decision I made to surrender my life to Jesus is why I am now walking into my destiny. He had been waiting for me with open arms.

Although I was terrified, I started walking by faith because He was leading me. The process of transformation was accomplished in my life through His love because Jesus is loving and compassionate.

His love has no limits, it has no boundaries, and it has no hidden agenda because His love is unconditional. The love that I was yearning for came from Jesus. His compassion and everlasting mercy towards me forgave my sins.

I found myself in a dark place without hope and Jesus took me out of that place through His eternal forever lasting mercy. His love moved me and made me a new person. The person that I was no longer existed. My family was able to notice something had changed in my life.

Love has a Name…JESUS

I told them I had Jesus in my heart and He filled me with His love. My parents quickly recognized that Jesus had performed a miracle in my life. I could no longer think, talk, or behave in the same way. I was a new creation; the old me was gone.

"I was a new creation; the old me was gone." 2 Corinthians 5:17

---

2 Corinthians 5:17 mentions,

"Therefore, if anyone is in Christ, he is a new creation; old things have passed away; behold, all things have become new" (NKJV). The scales that were blinding me were removed from my eyes. For the first time in my life, I could truly see. I no longer saw life with disappointments, pain, or hatred.

I began to view people with a love that I could not understand. I even demonstrated it towards individuals that had caused me disappointments. This was something I was unable to do before.

Many of the people that I held resentment and bitterness toward were telling me, *"There is something so different about you."* They would ask me, *"What happened to you?"* because they saw something different. All I could say to them was that Jesus saved me and I no longer felt the same way.

I would share my experience, and then I would tell them that Jesus' love touched and transformed my life. I also shared that I no longer felt the pain and hurt that had consumed me. Jesus' transformative power came in the form of an unmeasurable love.

I could have all the love I desired from the one who died on the cross for me. I really could not even perceive the magnitude of Him dying on the cross for me. Jesus endured disappointments from His very own people and the same people He left His Kingdom to save.

John 1:11 mentions, *"He came to his own, and his own people did not receive him"* English Standard Version (ESV). Jesus came from a Kingdom in which God's will was obeyed in totality (Matthew 6:10). In the same manner, God gave Adam the authority and dominion to execute in the Garden of Eden.

Adam, on the other hand, surrendered the dominion to Satan because of his disobedience unto God causing separation between God and man.

Thereafter, God sent His Son as part of His plan to redeem man again with the Father. Jesus came to earth to save and reconnect mankind with God.

"Jesus came to earth to save and reconnect mankind with God."

John 3:16 states,

"For God so loved the world that He gave His only begotten Son, that whoever believes in Him should not perish but have everlasting life" (NKJV).

God created man with a free will, which needs to be surrendered for God's will.

There is a feeling of amazement when I recall the day I said, "*I cannot do it on my own, I need you Jesus!*" The moment I gave my heart and will to my Savior I instantaneously experienced a transformation that until this day continues to be activated.

At that moment, I knew what I had always known; God had a purpose for my life. I was born again and was given a new opportunity and identity.

Although I could not express it at that moment, now I understand that through His love and infallible compassion was produced an evident change. I have always known I was destined for a great purpose, but it could only be achieved through His transformative love. It's amazing to be able to have an all-powerful God live within me, in this jar of clay!

I do not take it lightly in knowing that Jesus' Glory is reflected through my life. I was lost in my disillusions until I decided to give up my will unto Jesus.

My life was in chaos and to experience how He has turned my life around in such a powerful way leaves me in AWE. *"Being transformed by the blood of Jesus is undeniably the single most euphoric episode that I have ever encountered!"* (Edwin Burgos)

Jesus had waited years for me, yet it only took Him one powerful moment to execute the process of transformation.

Love has a Name…JESUS

A Moment of Reflection

Notes: _____

_____

_____

_____

_____

_____

Prayer

Lord Jesus, I pray that a transformation will occur in the life of the person who has read these pages. This transformation can only occur through Your loving power. I pray their lives will demonstrate to the world that You are still a miracle worker; Amen!

30

The Encounter

"With every new encounter with God your vision becomes clearer and sharper."
Sunday Adelaja

Chapter Two

As a child I recall being fascinated with drawing hearts and flowers. I wanted to see everybody in harmony with one another. However, as I began to experience challenges in my life, I soon realized that life was not as harmonious as I thought it should be.

I allowed the many disappointments to turn into bitterness and hatred; I no longer drew hearts and flowers. I was not mature enough to acquire the life experience needed to understand and accept that disappointments were going to occur, even from loved ones.

Love has a Name…JESUS

Due to my discontentment, I began to allow horrible thoughts to penetrate my mind. These discontents then began to dictate how I viewed life, especially my own.

Roman 12:2 states,

> *"Don't copy the behavior and customs of this world, but let God transform you into a new person by changing the way you think. Then you will learn to know God's will for you which is good and pleasing and perfect"* New Living Translation (NLT).

It is clear that Paul is emphasizing for the new believers not to adapt to their surroundings and environment.

God's will for the believers is to create His identity in their lives, which is good. God is a good God and will always have the best interest of His people. He wants believers to understand that it would please Him to see us become more like His Son, Jesus.

By allowing God's word to instruct and guide our daily lives, we would be doing the perfect will of God. All I knew was that I had to have control of my life and my surroundings, but soon I became exhausted and frustrated. I began to consume alcohol. It was readily available and something that I was familiar with because of my upbringing.

In my traditional Puerto Rican household, drinking alcohol during special occasions, or should I say any event, was considered very common. My parents did the best they could to provide and take care of their children. They worked hard, but could only achieve as far as life lessons taught them.

"My uncle, who answered the calling of God upon his life to be a missionary…was a person I looked up to and admired."

I always knew that I had a calling and purpose to work for the Kingdom of God. As a young girl, I attended church with my parents and sometimes with my grandmother. I loved being in church and experiencing the great feeling during the worship service.

My heart was always inclined towards the service of the Lord. My uncle, who answered the calling of God upon his life to be a missionary in Venezuela, was a person I looked up to and admired. The family would make sure to spread any news about my uncle and the work that he and his wife were doing in this foreign land.

I would say to myself, "*I want to be just like him and do something for God*". Life however would continue to knock me down; and with every blow I would be left gasping for air. Life had changed my heart towards people in ways I would never have expected. Once I allowed Jesus into my heart, then my healing process began.

As I look back on 1993, I remember being in distress and in rage with my life. I woke up one morning trying to be positive. I knew that I wanted to please God with a positive attitude and heart. I had not yet been filled with the Holy Spirit, although I knew I would not be able to go through this journey without Him.

I was invited to attend a church in Reading, Pennsylvania and after driving for three hours, I finally arrived at a traditional Pentecostal church. It was a brick and stained glass building that smelled faintly of mildew, and the sanctuary was on the second floor.

Love has a Name…JESUS

While I climbed the old wooden stairs that led to a small foyer, I felt nervous and anxious. There were three sections of dark wooden pews in this large old fashioned church. I entered a nearly empty sanctuary, occupied with only a couple of women and men praying before the beginning of the service.

At the front of the church, on the right side, sat the group of sisters that had invited me. I, however, sat on the right-side section next to the aisle. I found myself in an unfamiliar place with unfamiliar people. I thought to myself, "*What am I doing here, so far away from home, to attend a church service?*"

Suddenly, the church began to fill. The youth entered with smiles and laughter as they sat with their friends. I went unnoticed and began to observe the joy that emulated from them as they embraced one another.

A young girl began the service with a prayer, and what a prayer it was. She must have been in her late teens, but she knew how to pray with authority.

I felt every word that came out of her mouth. She was the worship leader and began to sing songs that had powerful and meaningful words. I felt as if she knew me and what I was feeling in my life.

I stood in the pew and said to myself, "*I feel so empty*". The music was loud and the anointing upon the worship leader filled the atmosphere, yet I still felt so alone and abandoned.

There I stood in the midst of so many young people, all joined in worship and singing along with the worship leader, but the feeling of emptiness kept me feeling sorry for myself.

"I wanted to praise God, but I felt inadequate and unworthy"

However, something inside of me wanted to scream out and do what the worship leader was doing, which was praising God! I could see that she had something special with Jesus. It was so evident in her demeanor, and her appearance was glowing and beautiful.

Through her voice, you could sense her love towards God. It filled me with the urge to shout and reach out for Him.

I wanted to praise God, but I felt inadequate and unworthy. There was something inside of myself telling me that I could never have or feel what she had.

> *"You argued with your husband before leaving your house…", "You left on bad terms…", "God is not going to hear you or forgive you…", "You are a hypocrite being here in the midst of all these people…"*

Condemnation was flooding my mind and at that time, I did not understand that there was no condemnation for those in Christ Jesus.

I was saved but had little knowledge of the Bible. Paul wrote about condemnation in Roman 8:1, *"So now there is no condemnation for those who are in Christ Jesus."*

I understood that this passage referred to Jesus Christ's sacrifice on the cross and His resurrection; it belongs to every person who accepts Jesus as their savior.

The old behaviors and thoughts are no longer ruling over the new believers, but the devil will try to discredit Jesus' atonement with deception by trying to convince believers that they are still in bondage. As I sat there, the preacher walked by me with other leaders.

Love has a Name...JESUS

I recognized a leader who had ministered to me a couple of months before at a youth event called "Summer Fest-1993". He was a humble man who knew God and moved in the prophetic. At that moment, I felt my inside tremble with fear as if he was going to single me out again.

"My heart was filled with beautiful feelings that were new to me."

I know now that it was the Holy Spirit tugging on my spirit to praise God. I began to worship God in a soundless voice. Soon after, I felt something released at that moment. As I continued to glorify God, I felt a liberation and I did not understand what was happening to me.

The more I praised, the more I cried. I was no longer embarrassed to worship God in a loud voice. I didn't even notice as I was releasing my praises, just like the worship leader had done at the beginning of the service.

At first, the tears that were released were of sadness and sorrow, but then I was no longer shedding tears of pain but of joy. I was feeling a love I had never experienced or felt before. I no longer felt empty.

My heart was filled with beautiful feelings that were new to me. I did not know what to do with myself, but I did know that I desired more of Him. All I wanted to do was praise God.

"I understand now that it was the beginning of my healing process."

Little did I know that there was a miracle with my name on it. I continued to cry as I opened my mouth to praise Him. As I cried, I began to feel free. The more I cried, the less angry and distressed I felt.

As the moments went by, a transformation occurred in my soul. I had no idea that I was being delivered and set free from all the pain and suffering.

Love has a Name…JESUS

For so many years, I had encountered so much pain that I cried for nearly an hour. It was all in God's plans because no one interrupted the work of the Holy Spirit within my heart. I had gone through so much, by myself, for so many years and Jesus knew I needed to cry. I understand now that it was the beginning of my healing process.

The Holy Spirit was preparing my heart for the Word that was going to be brought by this anointed young man. My mind, soul, and heart had to be ready because that night I would be required to make some critical and detrimental decisions that would affect the rest of my life.

The moment had arrived; I knew that I could never turn back. I had experienced an awesomeness that I had desired for so long, and I had finally obtained it.

The sermon was so powerful that I just couldn't wait for an altar call. I could not wait for the speaker to finish because the only thing I wanted to do was run to the altar, crying and thanking Jesus for what He had done for me on that night.

All it took was a moment with the power of the Holy Spirit. I left that place feeling like a new and transformed person. It was an intense and overpowering personal encounter with my Savior that I will never ever forget.

Love has a Name…JESUS

A Moment of Reflection

Notes: _____

_____

_____

_____

_____

_____

Prayer

Jesus, I now realize I have sinned against you. Please forgive me of my sins. Please come into my life and change my heart. I want you to be my Savior. In Jesus name, I pray. Amen. (Romans 8:9-10)

The Grace

"Grace means undeserved kindness. It is the gift of God to man the moment he sees he is unworthy of God's favor."
Dwight L. Moody

Chapter Three

From one moment to another, someone's entire world can change in a drastic way, and this is exactly what happened to me. I was deep into my problems, self-pity, and sin but by the grace of God I was set free.

I have to admit that I did not understand what had transpired inside of me. Through Jesus Christ, I became a daughter of the King of kings. I never thought I would be worthy, let alone that it could have happened to me. I was in turmoil for such a long time that my heart was full of resentment.

I was taught to fear God at a very young age and to believe in miracles. God to me was real but yet He seemed so far away.

Little did I know I would be filled with His indescribable and unexplainable love. He would soon begin the healing process for my deep resentment. I understood something had changed because I no longer talked or walked the same way; I viewed the world in a whole new way.

I realized that I had embraced and received the love that Jesus poured inside of me.

Roman 5:5 states

> "…*because God's love has been poured into our hearts through the Holy Spirit who has been given to us*" English Standard Version (ESV).

I was taught while attending church that one day Jesus would return for His Church.

I had a clear understanding of what the "Rapture" was and that when it happened the unbelievers would not be able to understand. This occurrence will shake the earth and it will happen in a blink of an eye.

The book of 1 Corinthians 15:52 mentions,

"It will happen in a moment, in the blink of an eye, when the last trumpet is blown. For when the trumpet sounds, those who have died will be raised to live forever. And we who are living will also be transformed" (NLT).

Paul writes to the Church of Corinth reaffirming that at any moment God will command for the trumpets to sound declaring Jesus to return and receive His bride, who is the Church.

"The Holy Spirit would remind me that the rapture was real, and Jesus was coming back."

I remember when I was not serving the Lord, there were nights when all the noise would cease and I could hear myself thinking. The Holy Spirit would remind me that the rapture was real, and Jesus was coming back.

All of sudden those thoughts would become so loud in

my mind that it would bring me fear of staying behind. All I wanted to do was remove those thoughts from my mind. The fear of knowing that I was living a life of sin shook me because I knew I was on my way to hell.

Fear is a human emotion that is triggered by a perceived threat. The possibility of staying behind and having to go through the "Tribulation" would set my mind into turmoil. Once I reconciled my life to Jesus, I no longer felt the fear of being left behind.

I faithfully know that I will spend eternity with my Savior. I think about the people who have not accepted Jesus into their hearts and it saddens me. There is still an opportunity for you to receive Jesus into your heart; today can be your day.

Fear can create powerful emotions in a person that can either paralyze or propel them into their destiny. Permitting fear to propel me into the unknown without understanding the process has allowed me to launch into a journey with God and to this day, I have no regrets.

Along with my fear, I had low self-esteem. Many times I would ask myself, *"What good am I?"*, *"What is my purpose in life?"* It was difficult to overcome all the negative emotions that were inside of me. I could not understand why life was so unfair. All I ever wanted was to please my husband and parents.

I would ask myself most often, *"What is wrong with me?"* For years, I was searching for answers that could only be found in God. I allowed myself to be a victim of self-pity. As I look back now, those difficult times made me feel like I had no value.

"I allowed myself to be a victim
of self-pity."

Those difficult times thrust me to seek my Savior. I needed rescuing and I was looking for it from my parents but specifically from my husband. However, I was unable to see that they also were in need of a Savior. They all had issues they were struggling with which they sought in empty places.

They were unable to give something that they also lacked; I was placing unrealistic expectations on them. As I look back, I can actually say, *"I was being unfair to them."* Goethe stated,

49

"It is the nature of grace to fill the places that have been empty."

Many times I felt my heart was an empty jar, lacking love because of the hurt I had encountered throughout my life. I became a cold and isolated woman, and many times, I felt like I had no life, just emptiness. No one knew what was in my heart.

I was lacking something in my life that I so desperately wanted, and I could only find it in the Lord. My heart could not produce something beautiful because it was consumed with resentment and bitterness.

Only God is able to search the depth of the heart. Jeremiah 17:10 mentions, *"But I, the Lord, search all hearts…"* (NLT). Indeed, Jesus flooded my emptiness with His Grace.

Additionally, another issue that I battled with was that I was barren; I was unable to produce the love that my loved ones deserved. I felt like I had nothing to give; I thought I had given my all. I did not know that barrenness generates loneliness.

Although I was surrounded by people, I still felt alone. In 1 Samuel 1:5 it states,

> *"But to Hannah, he would give a double portion, for he loved Hannah, although the Lord had closed her womb"* (NKJV).

God closed Hannah's womb? It almost sounds horrifying. She

loved her husband, and he loved her, but she was unable to give him a child.

Hannah's heart desired to produce a child, but she was barren. This situation would make her feel lonely because her husband had another wife named Peninnah, who gave birth to many children.

The feeling of emptiness inside of me lasted for many years, and the emptiness did not allow me to produce. Rick Warren stated,

> *"Your heart is designed to contain God. God wants to live inside of you but when your life is filled with other things, there's no room in your heart for God. This means you're not plugged into God's power and that's why you're tired all the time. And that's why you're stressed out all the time and that's why you worry all the time."* (Your Heart is Designed for God to Fill)

Jesus, my Savior who is the giver of life, breathed into mine and it happened through His amazing grace.

Hannah cried out to God, and He heard her. The word spoken by the High Priest over Hannah changed her life forever.

She came out of being barren and she gave birth to a

child. Wow, that is the power of an on time Word! God granted Hannah a son named Samuel and she dedicated him to God's service. Hannah finally was able to give her husband children and beside Samuel she gave birth to three sons and two daughters.

"I have not been the same since the day I surrendered my all."

Just like Hannah I received from God an on time Word. Jesus' sacrifice was the ultimate atonement that was promised since the fall of Adam and Eve. *"For God so loved the world, that he gave his only begotten Son, that whosoever believeth in him should not perish, but have everlasting life"* John 3:16 (KJV).

Once I embraced and accepted Jesus into my heart, His grace overtook me and immediately I fell in love with Him. God's Grace is Mind-Blowing states,

Love has a Name…JESUS

"Throughout the Scriptures, the message of this grace is proclaimed. Our God is "merciful and gracious, slow to anger, and abounding in steadfast love and faithfulness, keeping steadfast love for thousands, forgiving iniquity and transgression and sin" (Exodus 34:6-7). This grace is distinct to the Christian faith. No other religion emphasizes divine grace the way the Bible does." (Phillip Holmes)

I have not been the same since the day I surrendered my all.

I decided to serve the Lord with all my heart and I was not going to look back. Jesus began to remove the bitterness that for years took over my life.

Years have gone by, and I have not felt the pain that He uprooted. I will forever be grateful because of His grace. His love performed a miracle in my life that I never thought could have been possible. God had His eyes on me and I know for a fact that I will continue to experience His amazing grace.

I can't help to think about the song titled *"Amazing Grace"*. "Amazing Grace, how sweet the sound, that saved a wretched like me, I once was lost, but now am found, was blind, but now I see…"

A Moment of Reflection

Notes: _____

_____

_____

_____

_____

Prayer

Father God, I yearn to receive the Holy Spirit who will show me the power of the resurrection that will transform me to do Your will. Holy Spirit I want an overflow in my life. I want to be used by You and manifest Your gifting in the Kingdom of God. I ask all this in the name of Jesus. Amen!

The Suddenly

---

*"And suddenly there came a sound from heaven as of
a rushing mighty wind, and it filled all the house
where they were sitting."*
(Acts 2:2)

Chapter Four

I remember waking up one morning thinking to myself, "I'm tired of this life, and I can't take it anymore." I was tired of the life I was living and so dissatisfied. My life did not have meaning nor direction, but deep down in my heart I knew I had a purpose.

Little did I know that my life would soon change forever. Later that day, I was scheduled to go out of town to a youth event called "Summer Fest" in 1993. I was invited by my friend whom I have known since middle school. She was the vessel God chose to exhibit His love for me. I am so grateful for her friendship.

It was the first time I attended a youth event since I was 13 years of age. I accepted my friend's invitation to a four-hour drive because I wanted to get away from the oppressed environment I was living in. I was trying to forget the misery that I was going through.

"All I wanted was for the pain inside of me to go away."

I wanted to feel happy because there was a void inside my heart. No matter what I did, the void was still there. It was a constant reminder that something was missing.

I experienced a powerful encounter of the Holy Spirit upon my life on that hot summer evening in Monticello, NY at the Spanish Eastern District Mahanaim campground. God was waiting for me. I had never seen the power of God upon hundreds of youth in one place.

As we were driving to Monticello, I began to ponder on

my life up to that point. All I could see and think about was the miserable life I was living. All I wanted was for the pain inside of me to go away.

As I arrived to the event, I said to myself, *"What am I doing here?"*, not knowing that in the evening I was going to encounter something supernatural that would mark me for life.

As I was standing in the midst of young people filled with the Holy Spirit, I also began to sense His Presence. It was so overwhelming and tremendous that I wanted to praise God's Holy Name but I felt undeserving.

David Brazzeal mentions, *"Praise is the portal to the presence of God."* (Pray like a Gourmet: Creative Ways to Feed Your Soul) I began to struggle with the Holy Spirit as I was being convicted to forgive those who had disappointed me.

I had very little knowledge of the supernatural things of God. I knew that He was real, but I continued to struggle with His prompting, directing and instructing. The only thing I knew was that I wanted to cry because of all the immense pain and sorrow I had inside.

I could feel something happening within my heart. I wanted the pain to go away; I wanted to feel joy.

Romans 15:13 declares,

> *"Now may the God of hope fill you with all joy and peace in believing, that you may abound in hope by the power of the Holy Spirit"* (NKJV).

My mind couldn't understand or fathom what I was experiencing.

"I felt an emptiness that I believed no one would be able to fill."

I thought to myself, "*What just happened?*" My mind was struggling in the natural sense trying to understand the supernatural but to no avail (Isaiah 55:8-9). During the course of the service, I felt an emptiness that I believed no one would be able to fill.

I decided towards the end of the event to surrender my life to Jesus and allow Him to take control.

"What we really need is only a heart of surrender & always trust what God has plan for our life. So we do our best, God shall take the rest; That's what I called Faith." (Olivia Sinaga, Goodreads)

I surrendered not knowing what was going to happen next in my life but I had to trust God to be in control.

Suddenly, Jesus' unconditional love overpowered my life and I was overwhelmed with a whole different set of emotions. I was unable to speak, and all I could do was cry.

According to Acts 2:2,

"And suddenly there came a sound from heaven as of a rushing mighty wind, and it filled all the house where they were sitting" (KJV).

I was being filled with the Holy Spirit but in my human mind I was unable to conceive what was occurring.

I would like to define the word, *"suddenly"*. According to the Webster Dictionary, *"Suddenly"* means an unexpected manner; unexpectedly; hastily; without preparation. In Hebrew, the word moment, *"Raga"*, means *suddenly* just like in the Day of Pentecost. In Acts 2:2 states, *"Suddenly…filled all the house where they were sitting."*

Love has a Name...JESUS

Before Jesus was taken into heaven, He told the disciples to wait for the Holy Spirit (Acts 1:4). Even though the disciples and witnesses watched Jesus ascend into the sky, they did not know when they were going to receive the filling of the Holy Spirit.

Jesus told them to wait and for them not to leave Jerusalem. Then on the day of Pentecost, the God moment happened, they received their *"suddenly"*. The unexpected experience happened and their lives were never the same.

"I embraced His love and peace without any reservations."

Gary Wilkerson article indicates,

> *"Jesus is promising them, "God desires those changes for you, but such things only happen through the power of the Spirit. Until he comes, things will remain the same."* (Wait On the Holy Spirit Article)

Love has a Name…JESUS

All I knew was that a *"suddenly"* had occurred in my life.

Jesus not only filled me with His love but also His peace that surpasses all understanding Philippians 4:7 indicates, *"and the peace of God, which surpasses all understanding, will guard your hearts and minds through Christ Jesus"* (NKJV).

I embraced His love and peace without any reservations. It had been years that I was searching and searching for love and peace like I was experiencing. My spirit man came to life because it was finally connected with the Spirit of God.

I had no idea that I was going to encounter experiences with God that would transform my life.
Rick Warren states,

> *"Transformation is a process, and as life happens there are tons of ups and downs. It's a journey of discovery – there are moments on mountaintops and moments in deep valleys of despair."*

The fulfillment in my heart was what I needed in order to become alive and be able to see that my life had purpose.

Jesus came to earth for the helpless and hopeless and is near to the broken hearted. Psalms 34:18 indicates, *"The Lord is near to those who have a broken heart, and saves such as have a contrite spirit"* (NKJV).

Jesus is not only in the past but also in the present time; He wants to work in our lives **"*now*"**.

In Isaiah 41:10 it states,

> *"Fear not, for I am with you; be not dismayed, for I am your God; I will strengthen you, I will help you, I will uphold you with my righteous right hand"* (ESV).

I no longer had to feel alone, helpless and hopeless because His righteous right hand was going to sustain me.

"True and absolute freedom is only found in the presence of God."

Jesus continues to be available right now. He was telling me, "*I am with you*", and it offered me security and comfort. I understood that I no longer had to protect myself because He became my protector. I no longer had to walk alone because He would be with me until the end of time.

Wow, a "*suddenly of God*" can arrive at any time in a

person's life. My suddenly happened in the summer of 1993, and my life has never been the same. Jesus' presence became tangible to me. *"True and absolute freedom is only found in the presence of God"* (Aiden Wilson Tozer). In the presence of God there is fullness of love, peace and joy.

I continue to have pivotal moments in my journey with the Lord that have marked me in ways that I never thought possible.

My natural mind could not comprehend, but my spirit had been connected to the All Powerful God. So you see, expect the unexpected, the *"suddenly"*, because at any moment the Holy Spirit will embrace and fulfill you.

A Moment of Reflection

Notes: _____

_____

_____

_____

_____

_____

Prayer

Lord Jesus, I want to encounter a "suddenly moment" with
You that will change my perspective of who You are in
my life. In the name of Jesus!
Amen!

The Vision

"Healing doesn't mean the damage never existed. It means the damage no longer controls your life…"
Akshay Dubey

Chapter Five

Ever since I was very young, I would experience attacks in my dreams. These dreams would cause me fear and torment. The encounters I had as I slept were not of this world but from the supernatural realm.

Even though I lacked knowledge in God's Word and in the supernatural, I knew one thing, I was set apart for a specific calling in the Kingdom of God.

Deep down within my heart, I always knew that God had a purpose and plan for my life. The seed of the Gospel had been planted in my heart from a very young age through my parents and grandmother. Luke 8:11 mentions, *"Now the parable is this: The seed is the word of God"* (NKJV).

However, with no one to nourish the seed that was planted, it became dormant and remained in that phase for many years. In June of 1993, I decided to re-dedicate my life to Jesus Christ and the seed was reborn again. I felt as if I'd come out of a deep sleep. The Holy Spirit breathed life into my soul. Genesis 2:7 states,

> *"Then the LORD God formed a man from the dust of the ground and breathed into his nostrils the breath of life, and the man became a living being"* (NKJV).

I could not explain it, but I knew something had awakened inside of me and I felt like a new person.

God's supernatural power began to dwell inside my heart causing the seed that had been planted to grow. A seed will go through a process before bearing fruit. The scientific name for this process is called germination. The seeds come in different shapes and sizes. There are basic elements that are crucial for the seed and its growth.

The seed will need soil, water, light, the correct temperature and time in order for the germination to take place.

The seeds are planted first in order for the roots to attach themselves to the soil. Once these roots are attached, a small plant will begin to emerge and eventually break through the soil. This process is called germination of the seed.

"The seeds are planted first in order for the roots to attach themselves to the soil."

The germination process that a seed goes through can be compared to the process of a new believer. The seed is Jesus' DNA that has been injected in a new believer's life with the goal being to develop the character of Christ.

The Word of God is the fertile ground in which the seed can produce and deepen its roots in order to receive the necessary nutrients.

In the book of Matthew 13:23 it states,

"But he who received seed on the good ground is he who hears the word and understands it, who indeed bears fruit and produces: some a hundredfold, some sixty, some thirty" (NKJV).

This helps the believer to obtain instructions and guidance in order to have a healthy spiritual growth.

The Word of God should be the core in all believers' lives. The amount of light is also essential for the seed to grow, and the scripture declares that Jesus is the light of the world.

"Then Jesus spoke to them again, saying, 'I am the light of the world. He who follows Me shall not walk in darkness, but have the light of life'" (John 8:12,

NKJV).

Jesus lights the way for believers through His Word, which is a light unto our path.

The Word of God is also referred to as the Truth. Submission to the Truth (Word) will bring clarity to the believer when unable to see his/her way. The temperature where the seed will germinate is also vital for growth, just like in the life of the believer.

In the same manner that the temperature needs to be hot in the process of germination, it should also be applied to a believer's prayer life. This will provoke to be in the presence of God which will produce intimacy and spiritual growth.

The believer will go through trials in life, but if they applied these elements in their daily lives, they will grow their roots deep into the Word of God.

"I laid there silent without being able to say a word."

Henceforth, the evidence of the believers' fruits will be visible. Matthew 7:16 declares, "*You will know them by their fruits...*" (NKJV). I knew that the walk was not going to be easy, especially the restoration of my marriage of 11 years. I remember so vividly one early morning about 6 o'clock, I woke up from a disturbing dream that was related to a betrayal from my past.

As I woke up, I felt my heart beating so fast that I began to perspire. I could not think clearly nor focus because the pain was strong within my heart. The feeling that I was experiencing felt as if the dream was real.

I was trying to catch my breath and tried to calm down. I laid there silent without being able to say a word. I thought to myself, *"It was only a dream."*

I began to ask the Lord, *"Oh no, the pain again? It felt so real."* I had a misconception that once I was saved all my past problems would disappear. I thought my life and everything around me was going to be okay. I would never have to feel any more pain or sorrow. I was horribly mistaken!

At that particular moment, I began to feel strange but it was not in a bad way. It was actually a peaceful feeling. I was unable to express what was occurring.

All of a sudden, this presence filled my heart and it began to consume me and started to sooth my mind. The room was still dark. I was facing the ceiling with my eyes closed.

Unexpectedly, I began to see right through the roof of the house and then I saw the sky and all the stars. The cosmos began to shift and the sky began to separate creating a detachment from the natural world to the supernatural world.

The color of the sky, which was a dark blue, began to

lighten up as the separation was taking place. I was in awe, and I did not want to move a muscle in my body. I was afraid that what I was seeing would end. My husband was sleeping right next to me.

"He was wearing a radiant white mantle around His head and His robe illuminated."

I wanted to wake him up but I could not speak a word. I was so intrigued and at the same time in awe of what was happening. I was witnessing something that was literally out of this world.

I sometimes think back on that early morning experience and how God allowed this imperfect woman to see His Greatness; it's beyond my understanding. The God who created the heavens and the earth was showing me His awesome wonders.

All of sudden, I was staring at a huge window and

everything was so bright and white.

I began to see the most beautiful Person who was standing between two men. I knew who He was by the way my heart began to leap with excitement. He was wearing a radiant white mantle around His head and His robe illuminated. As much as I tried to see His face, I was unable.

Without noticing that the radiance that flowed from His face was so pure that it produced healing within me. He then asked me, *"Do you feel the pain?"*, I said in a still low voice, *"No, I don't feel the pain."* In that instant, the pain of betrayal and disappointments that for so many years had me bounded, disappeared!

Jesus had healed and set my heart free. I was in awe and began to cry, not of sadness but of joy.

For years, I had tried with my own strength to get rid of the pain in my heart, but I was unsuccessful. I was serving the Lord with all my heart, mind and soul, however, every time I had a dream or a thought, the pain would resurface. I thought the pain would cease once I invited Jesus into my heart.

I had to learn that there is a designated time for everything. It did not happen when I wanted it to happen. It happened at the right time through a beautiful vision I had with Jesus. Jesus allowed me to experience something so majestic and sublime. I continue to say, *"Lord, the pain of betrayal and disappointments disappeared in an instant."*

Since that day, I have continued to receive healing in other areas of my life. Years have passed by since I had that vision in that early morning, but I will never forget the manner that He healed the pain in my heart.

A supernatural experience with Jesus will bring transformation to a person's life that needs change since we are unable to do it on our own.

The book of Hebrews, chapter 13 and verse 8 declares, *"Jesus has not changed, He is the same yesterday, today and forever"* (NKJV). I have learned that my life belongs to Him. My relationship is based on who He is in my life.

Jesus yearns for His creation to seek Him for who He is and not for what He is able to provide. Seek Him first, and His Kingdom and everything else will fall into place in due time (Matthew 6:33).

As you spend time with Jesus, you will begin to trust and strengthen your relationship with Him. Jesus is waiting for you.

A Moment of Reflection

Notes: _____

_____

_____

_____

_____

_____

Prayer

Jesus, before You ascended to heaven You Promised that we would receive the Holy Spirit who is our Counselor. I'm asking for the Holy Spirit to fill me with His power so that I may be changed from the inside out. In the mighty name of Jesus. (Acts 2) Amen!

The Dream

---

*"Who are you to get a message from God while you sleep?
Well, why not you? God sometimes uses dreams to
communicate— and he May do so for
anyone who's paying attention."*
Whitney Hopler

Chapter Six

One of my experiences with the Holy Spirit was a God dream. I call it a God dream in order to differentiate from a regular dream. A God dream to me is when God is sharing a message while I am asleep.

In this particular dream, I saw myself in a huge building, in a beautiful foyer, and on the main floor where there were many people walking around. They seemed to be in a hurry because they were walking right by me without noticing that I was looking at them.

They seemed to be in a rush, focusing and trying to reach

their destination. I was sitting in a lovely round cushioned sitting area right in the center of the foyer. The sitting area was very comfortable and peaceful, even though I was in the midst of so many people.

"I could sense an overwhelming love that was flowing out of Him."

I was sitting all by myself when suddenly I felt a presence next to me. Quickly, I noticed a man sitting right next to me. It took me by surprise, which it shouldn't have because there were so many people in this huge foyer. I said to myself, *"Who is this man?"*

I realized that my heart was racing, and I could not understand why. The man sitting next to me did not speak a word; He stood there silently.

I could not see His entire face, only His eyes. I could sense an overwhelming love that was flowing out of Him. Apostle Paul writes in the book of Romans 5:5,

> *"and hope does not disappoint, because the love of God has been poured out within our hearts through the Holy Spirit who was given to us"* (NKJV).

My heart was full of immense excitement and astonishment.

His presence overshadowed my mind because I was unable to put my words together. All of a sudden our eyes met and I could feel His eyes piercing right through mine into my heart.

His eyes were full of unconditional and pure love. *Could it be Him? Could it be the one who rescued me from the dark place I found myself living for years? Could this be Jesus?"*

Jack Wellman wrote in an article about agape and stated,

> *"This is the Greek word for love at its ultimate. It is the most self-sacrificing love that there is. This type of love is the love that God has for His own children. This type of love is what was displayed on the cross by Jesus Christ. In John 3:16 it is written that "God so loved (agape) the world that He gave His only begotten Son that whoever believes in Him shall not perish but*

have everlasting life. Agape love is that which is always associated with the love of God and rarely does it occur when it involves one person in relations with another. The Greek word agape was hardly ever used in Greek-speaking societies but in the New Testament, it occurs 320 times" (What is Agape love? 2104).

"Even when we were dead because of our sins, He made us alive by what Christ did for us…" (Ephesians 2:5)

I knew from the beginning who He was because no one has ever been able to fill my soul with such a love and peace that's surpassed all understanding.

In Philippians 4:7 scripture declares,

"and the peace of God, which surpasses all understanding, will guard your hearts and minds through Christ Jesus" (NKJV).

Love has a Name…JESUS

No one has been able to love me the way Jesus has loved me. No one has ever cared enough to die on the cross for my sins. *"Even when we were dead because of our sins, He made us alive by what Christ did for us. You have been saved from the punishment of sin by His loving-favor"* (Ephesian 2:5, NLT).
His loving-favor saved me even though I was not worthy of it. Jesus was sitting right next to me.

The Holy One was next to me and looking at me with such tenderness and love. Isaiah 43:15 mentions, *"I am the Lord, your Holy One, The Creator of Israel, your King"* (NKJV).

At that moment no one else mattered or existed, it was just Jesus and me. You may wonder why a Great and Holy God would choose to sit next to someone whose made countless mistakes and shortcomings. In the book of Romans 3:23 indicates, *"For all have sinned, and come short of the glory of God"* (KJV).

Jesus is the reason I was able to experience an unconditional love that overtook my life and transformed it even with my deficiencies. I love the fact that because of His sacrifice and resurrection, He is sitting at the right hand of the Father making intercession for us (Romans 8:34 (NKJV).

I can rest assured that His righteousness has covered my life. I could not bring my eyes to turn away from His because I wanted to cherish the moment as long as I could. My heart was filled with His love towards me.

I continued my attempt to see the rest of His face but failed because of His radiance. All I was able to see was His loving eyes that are full of grace and mercy. *"Grace, mercy, and peace from God the Father and Christ Jesus our Lord"* (2 Tim. 1:2 NKJV).

"When you are intimate with someone else, you trust them enough to share your secrets…"

God's love towards His creation is indescribable. Human beings are so limited and are unable to understand His love. God created us to have fellowship with Him on a daily basis in order for us to establish an intimate relationship.

Love has a Name…JESUS

My desire was to build a close relationship with Jesus but at times it was difficult to do because of my lack of trust. The article on How to Have an Intimate Relationship with God states,

> *"When you are intimate with someone else, you trust them enough to share your secrets. As God, Jesus already knows everything about you anyway, but when you choose to tell him what's hidden deep within you, it proves you trust him. Trust is hard. You've probably been betrayed by other people, and when that happened, maybe you swore you'd never open up again. If you want the closest of relationships with God, you have to risk opening your heart. There's no other way. When you share yourself in relationship with Jesus, when you talk to him often and step out in faith, he will reward you by giving you more of himself. Stepping out takes <u>courage</u>, and it takes time. Held back by our fears, we can move beyond them only through the encouragement of the <u>Holy Spirit</u>."* (Principles for Growing in Your Relationship with God and Jesus Christ)

I had to learn how to trust God in order to obtain a relationship with God.

Nevertheless, I now understand that I am able to experience and encounter Jesus' love on a personal level on a daily basis. I will never be able to forget how my Godly dream filled me with His pure love. *"We love Him because He first loved us"* (1 John 4:19, NKJV). Jesus' love is able to change a person's life from the inside-out.

For so many years, I searched for love because I was in dire need of it. I was always seeking for someone or something to fill my heart with love.

"I was a new creation; the old me was gone." (2 Corinthians 5:17)

I searched for unconditional love in my husband, parents, and family but they were all limited.

According to Mahoney (2018),

> *"When we love unconditionally, and when we receive unconditional love, we find that there is power in those feelings*

and actions. We find hope. We find courage. Things we never knew to expect come from giving to one another of one another without any expectations." (Bible Versus on Unconditional Love, section: Unconditional Love is Powerful)

I also learned that I was limited and caused pain and rejection towards my love ones.

I struggled constantly not wanting to open my heart to them because I did not want to be disappointed. The Holy Spirit taught me that they didn't want to hurt me; they loved me despite the disappointments.

My family lacked the knowledge in the demonstration of their affection but deep down inside, I knew they loved me.

This is the reason why I had to ask them to forgive me for placing high expectations on them. Uma Thurman says it very well, *"But I think it is always difficult to have high expectations of yourself or anyone else."*

God is the only One that can fill a person's void. I had set a high expectation on people who I believed would be able to fill the emptiness that I had, however, I was wrong. I came to a realization that through this God dream, Jesus was able to change my perspective on how I viewed people and how limited we are.

Finally, I will never forget His loving eyes and piercing gaze that for the duration of the dream caused my heart to be filled with His Amazing Presence.

A Moment of Reflection

Notes: _____

_____

_____

_____

_____

Prayer

Father God, I pray that every person will be able to dream and meet You as a loving God. My desire is for each and every one of them to become intimate with You. Being in Your presence will mark their lives and create a hunger and thirst for Your righteousness. Amen!

The Hope

"For I know the thoughts that I think toward you, says the LORD, thoughts of peace and not of evil, to give you a future and a hope."
Jeremiah 29:11

Chapter Seven

During my early walk with the Lord there were times of spiritual highs in the Holy Spirit's presence. I had renounced to the practices that temporarily made me feel happy.

I had a real encounter through my personal experience with Christ Jesus especially when the Holy Spirit would visit me during my prayer time. I would be able to sense His presence in a tangible way. There were times during my personal devotions when I would experience deliverance and healing from things that occurred in my past. The presence of God is holy and it is a personal experience for each person who enters.

Love has a Name…JESUS

I always knew that my hope would be in Jesus, and I just needed to surrender my will unto Him. I knew that I would be encountering trials and disappointments throughout my walk with God.

Nonetheless, I will not be confronting them alone because I have the help of the Holy Spirit. Psalms 39:7 states, *"And now, Lord, what do I wait for? My hope is in You."* The Holy Spirit was teaching me through the scriptures that my hope is in the Lord.

He assured me that He would strengthen me through the present and future hardships.

At first I didn't have any issues with reading and trying to apply the Word of God in my daily walk. I was experiencing God in so many different ways, such as miracles, healings, deliverance, and restoration in relationships. I was constantly seeking the Presence of the Lord.

I witnessed God do great and mighty things in my home, family and close friends. There were times that I felt like I was walking on air.

The first year of my walk with Jesus was filled with amazing life changing experiences. The Holy Spirit revealed to me the love that Jesus had for me. There were times when my heart felt like it was going to burst.

However, the process required for spiritual maturity is not only needed during prayer time but also in studying the scriptures and serving others.

_____

"I had to learn how to depend
on the Word of God."

_____

I believe that the Holy Spirit was guiding me to encounter Him in a unique way. In the fall of 1993, my husband was laid off from his job where he had worked for 11 years. He was the bread winner in our family. My husband did not worry nor did he complain. He would say, *"God will provide."*

As for me, on the other hand, I began to worry and question God, *"Why?"* God was trying to teach me to walk by faith and not by my feelings (2 Corinthians 5:7, NKJV). I had to learn to depend on the Word of God. Soon after I understood that my hope comes from Christ, He would be the One to carry me through the hardships.

Now, I was no longer experiencing the Holy Spirit the way I was accustomed to during my devotion time. God was trying to teach me that I needed to depend on Him through His Word.

However, I wanted to feel His presence like I had felt it before. I didn't want to go a day without feeling His Holy Spirit. Steven J. Cole explains it like this,

> *"Spiritual highs are wonderful, but you can't live on them. You must learn to walk by faith, to be consistent in the Word, and to gather regularly with other believers to build one another in the things of God."*

I needed to study the Word of God and walk in obedience according to it.

Walking by faith is believing without having to know and see the results, and that was difficult for me to do. I remember reading the Bible one morning and coming across this scripture that spoke to my heart. *"Therefore do not worry about tomorrow, for tomorrow will worry about its own things. Sufficient for the day is its own trouble"* (Matthew 6:34, NKJV).

I was worrying and being impatient in my process because I wanted a fast solution.

God has His perfect timing and He will not entertain anyone's tantrums. I needed to wait on God to step in and provide a solution. The waiting period in the beginning of my walk with Jesus was difficult.

"I had to learn to wait on the Lord and His guidance in my decision making."

I was so used to being self-sufficient that if I needed to do something or take care of something, I would.
Isiah 40:31 states,

"But, while waiting on the Lord I got tired many times inpatient that I would become upset. Yet those who wait for the LORD Will gain new strength; They will mount up with wings like eagles, they will run and not get tired, they will walk and not become weary" (New American Standard Bible (NASB).

I had to learn to wait on the Lord and His guidance in my decision making.

There were many times I felt like taking matters into my hands, but I had to fight myself not to. I have to admit, I had to learn not to resist even though it was challenging. The more I submitted to God's guidance through His Word, the more I trusted Him.

Trust was another area in my life that needed to be addressed because I did not trust people. Trusting without knowing the details took its toll on me because that meant I was not in control.

The Holy Spirit wanted for me to recognize and accept that He was in control. Life's disappointments could have detained my process, but the promises of God would give me the hope I needed. The challenges of life can be a killer of hope.

However, the Holy Spirit who dwells inside of me would not allow me to forget that Christ is my hope. Colossians 1:27 tells us plainly, "*It is Christ in you, the hope of glory*" (NKJV).

In my times of trials, I often say in my prayer time, *"All it takes is to be in Your Presence."* In those moments, I have felt alone and forsaken but the Scripture would remind me, "…*I will never leave you nor forsake you*" Hebrew 13:5 (NKJV).

I have to admit, there were times I did not think I was going to make it but the Holy Spirit would empower me to believe that at any moment He would intervene and I would obtain the victory.

"Draw close to God and God will draw close to you..." James 4:8

There were also moments during my process that I felt alone during the trials. The feeling of being alone would try to consume me, but the anticipation of being in the presence of God would encourage me to continue to hope.

I knew it would take God's presence to give me the strength to continue walking in His promises. I was designed to spiritually prosper and endure life's trials. My heavenly Father promised that He would be with me and would not leave me alone to face the challenges of life.

God wanted for me to develop a closer relationship with Him, especially in the moments that I felt alone. James 4:8 says, "*Draw close to God and God will draw close to you…*" (NKJV). Jesus Christ understood loneliness as He was on the cross and He was separated from the Father.

He understands exactly how we feel when we are experiencing loneliness. I went through disillusions in the past that caused me to feel alone but I now understand that its part of life.

As a daughter of the King, I know I can come into His presence because I have access through Jesus Christ.
The Son has given unto me all the Father has given unto the Son.

> *"And the glory which You gave Me I have given them, that they may be one just as We are one:* ²³ *I in them, and You in Me; that they may be made perfect in one, and that the world may know that You have sent Me, and have loved them as You have loved Me"* (John 17:22-23, NKJV).

Jesus is hope and His promises are true.

Love has a Name…JESUS

The Holy Spirit has taught me that I need to continue to hope even through my trials, disappointments and loneliness.

"Our world today so desperately hungers for hope, yet uncounted people have almost given up. There is despair and hopelessness on every hand. Let us be faithful in proclaiming the hope that is in Jesus." (Billy Graham)

A Moment of Reflection

Notes: _____

_____

_____

_____

_____

Prayer

*My Lord Jesus Christ, don't allow anyone to lose hope in You. If
they feel they have lost hope for life, I pray that through the power
of Your Word they may receive it, right now.
In the name of Jesus.
Amen!*

Final words from the Author

The purpose in writing this book, *"Love has a Name…Jesus"*, was to invite the readers into my personal experiences with Jesus Christ. My prayer is that as every person reads through my experiences that it creates a desire to seek Him like never before in order to receive inner healing and deliverance.

Jesus came to earth to die on the cross for each and every one on this earth. God, the Father, gave His Only Beloved Son, not only to die on the cross and give us salvation, but also to set the captives free and heal the brokenhearted. In Luke 4:18 states, *"…He has sent Me to heal the brokenhearted, to proclaim liberty to the captives…"* (NKJV).

My desperation for peace of mind and answers to my problems drove me to call out to Jesus. I tried to resolve my problems with my own strength, but I failed with every attempt. The Lord heard my cry and came to my rescue.

I can assure you that if you are depleted by trying to work out your problems and it seems to get worse, I urge you to call on the name of Lord and I know that He will come and save you. As you draw closer to Him, you will begin to experience God like never before. *"Draw near to God and He will draw near to you..."* (James 4:8).

Transformation through Love

I wanted to quote people who have influenced my life and that in one way or another have contributed to my spiritual growth through inner healings and deliverances.

There are more people that I hold dear to my heart that has also imparted and planted in my heart the Love of God. They all have served so that God may be exalted and glorified in my life through their example.

I asked them to describe in their own words their thoughts about the transformation that occurs in a person's life through the power of Jesus' Love.

"It's a change that takes place in a person's life from the inside out."

Domiason Centeno
Evangelist and Outreach Ministries

"Every one of us who have had an encounter with Jesus knows the power of transformation. A clear example is the demon-possessed man from Gerasenes, who came to Jesus naked and uncontrollable and Jesus transformed the man and sent him back to his family. No one who visits the cross of Jesus will be the same again."

Juan A. Vera
Teacher of the Word

"In this journey we call life we have faced and will face challenging moments. Not just hardships but intense suffering, the kind that feels like you're going to die because the pain is so profound. In the midst of that kind of suffering, God calls us to love deeply in 1 Peter 4:8 "...because deep love covers a multitude of sins." It covers my faults and your issues and all the ugliness hiding within our soul surfaces not because God wants to shame us but because the Lord loves us with a deep love the kind of deep love that bore our sins. When we experience that love and extend that love we are transformed; our lives are never the same."

Dr. Joanne Solis-Walker
Assistant Dean of Global Theological Education & Director of Education for Latin's at Seminario Wesley en Indiana Wesleyan University

Love has a Name…JESUS

"Transformation is a progressive intentional transition to another level with purpose. The question is "Who's doing the transformation?"

Albert Torres
Presbyter, South Jersey/Delaware Section and
Senior Pastor, Hammonton Spanish Church A/G, NJ

"Every believer joining the body of Christ will begin to be transformed and processed until Christ is formed in their life; then they will be able to say, "I'm crucified with Christ, and I no longer live because Christ lives in me," and that is called the power of transformation."

Tomas Acevedo
Senior Pastor, Vineland Spanish Church A/G, NJ

"The power of love is reflected in the service and has the ability to change a life without expressing any words. A life touched by pure love will give by grace what she or he has received by grace, and the chain reaction of transformation will have no end."

Chaney García
Pastor, Restauración Total, Los Ángeles, CA

Love has a Name… Jesus

Seven Day Devotion

The Transformation

Transformation is a powerful force. In order to see transformation in your life, one of the most important components is to establish a life of prayer. It has to be a desire and need for your life. Jesus yearns to talk to you and you to Him.

He wants to demonstrate to you that the price He paid on the Cross of Calvary was to connect you to the Father in order to re-establish relationship, communion and fellowship with Him. A life of prayer will do exactly that! It will connect God, Jesus and the Holy Spirit to you. I do not know about you but there must be a life of prayer and intimacy with Jesus.

Along with a prayer life you must be dedicated and honest in your conversations with Jesus in order to see transformation. T.D. Jakes once said, *"Radical change comes only through our consistent efforts, honesty and dedication. To change something, we must be willing to see it clearly."* I urge you if you want to see yourself transformed you must seek God with all your heart; mark my word, you will receive a life-changing transformation.

Love has a Name…JESUS

"Then you will call upon Me and go and pray to Me, and I will listen to you. And you will seek Me and find Me, when you search for Me with all your heart." Jeremiah 29:12-13

PRAYER

Father God in the name of Jesus, I want to know You and I understand that it can be done by establishing a prayer life with You. Help me to be consistent and purposeful when I come into Your Presence. In Jesus Name, Amen

What is God telling you?

_____

_____

_____

_____

The Encounter

Having an encounter with Jesus Christ will mark you for life. You cannot experience Jesus and remain the same; that just does not happen. The meaning of encounter is defined by Webster dictionary as an "unexpected experience with someone".

You must seek Jesus through prayer and Scriptures consistently with an expectation that He will encounter you. Do not give up if it does not happen, but rather, continue to press on through for your encounter with Jesus. It will happen when you least expect it because He, and only He, knows the day and time.

The 3 Life-Changing Truths to Know About Encounters with God states, *"God is in the small things and He's in the big things. God Encounters look different for each one of us"* (Maggio, n.d.). Remember that the way His encounter was with me it will be different with you.

Jesus knows your heart and as you pursue Him, you will be visited by Him.

Love has a Name…JESUS

"and He who searches the hearts knows what the mind of the Spirit is, because He intercedes for the saints according to the will of God." Romans 8:27

PRAYER

My Lord Jesus Christ, I come before You understanding that You know all things and You know my heart. I want to have an unexpected experience because I do not want to be the same. I need You to help me because I am unable to do it on my own. Thank you for loving me unconditionally, in the name of Jesus I pray. Amen

What is God telling you?

_____

_____

_____

_____

The Grace

The grace of God is only obtained through the sacrifice of Jesus Christ on the Cross of Calvary. Many times you are unable to receive God's grace because you won't embrace that you have been forgiven.

You allow your past sins, errors or guilt to keep you under condemnation. Romans 8:1 mentions, *"There is therefore now no condemnation to those who are in Christ Jesus, who do not walk according to the flesh, but according to the Spirit."*

The only way to be in the Presence of God is for you to draw closer to God but you must let go of anything that can hold you back from entering into His Presence.

Jesus' assignment on earth was to reconnect, reconcile and redeem humanity to the Father. The faith and hope of obtaining salvation and being able to dwell in eternity with God is something that can only be attained through the Son; and with a clear understanding that His Grace is sufficient for you. *"God's mercy and grace give me hope – for myself, and for our world."* Billy Graham

Love has a Name…JESUS

"And the Word became flesh and dwell among us, and we beheld His glory, the glory as of the only begotten of the Father, full of grace and truth." John 1:14

PRAYER

Father God, please help me to not allow condemnation to hinder my hope and faith in You and in Your sacrifice on the Cross of Calvary. I want to receive Your amazing grace that has reconnected me to the Father. Amen!

What is God telling you?

_____

_____

_____

_____

The Suddenly

A sudden moment in your life with Jesus will change you from the inside out. There will not be any room for doubts or confusion. The evidence will be in the way your life will be revolutionized.

Paul, on his way to persecute the Christians, had a sudden moment in the book of Acts 9:3-4 which declares,

> *"As he journeyed he came near Damascus, and suddenly a light shone around him from heaven. The he fell to the ground, and heard a voice saying to him, "Saul, Saul, why are you persecuting Me?"* (NKJV)

That sudden moment left Paul blinded, but his perception was changed instantly after his experience.

Your sudden moment is going to be a life altering experience. Paul was blinded by His own understanding, but through Jesus Christ, Paul was able to see. Once you have an experience with Jesus where you become a renewed person, all you will have is gratitude towards His love and sacrifice.

"Then Jesus spoke to them again, saying, "I am the light of the world. He who follows Me shall not walk in darkness, but have the light of life." John 8:12 (NKJV)

PRAYER

Lord Jesus, I do not want to remain in a state of blindness in my own way. I want to see You and be able to be transformed into who You want me to be. I give my will to You so that Your will in my life can be done. In the name of Jesus. Amen

What is God telling you?

_____

_____

_____

_____

The Vision

God can use any method to speak to you and one of those is through visions. Dreams and visions are different, dreams are manifested while a person is sleeping and visions are given when the person is awake.

Visions should always coincide with the scriptures, the Word of God, in order to understand the vision in a clearer way. If you are unable to interpret the vision, you should ask God for wisdom and interpretation. James 1:5 indicates,

> *"If any of you lacks wisdom, let him ask God, who gives generously to all without reproach, and it will be given him."*

So ask God for wisdom in order to interpret a vision or a message that is unclear to you.

God is faithful and will equip you with the wisdom to understand the message He is trying to relate to you. I urge to ask the Holy Spirit to speak to you through visions; but do not limit Him on the methods he does choose to use.

"And it shall come to pass afterward, that I will pour out My Spirit on all flesh; Your sons and your daughters shall prophesy, your old men shall dream dreams, your young men shall see visions." Joel 2:28

PRAYER

I want to be able to have an experience through visions and to receive a message from you that will transform my life. I believe You speak in many different ways. I also understand that the Bible tell us everything we need to know. Thank you, Jesus for Your Word.

What is God telling you?

_____

_____

_____

_____

The Dream

Breathitt is a well-known teacher of the Scriptures and he states, that God uses dreams to provide us with messages, but also, to show us His plans and purpose for our lives. (Dream Interpretation According to the Bible)

If you have not experienced a dream from God, all you have to do is begin to ask the Holy Spirit to give you one. Sometimes we do not have dreams because we don't ask. I remember asking God to speak to me however He wanted to and He did. I was not so concerned in the method, I just wanted to hear from Him. He did it through the Scriptures, people, to my heart and dreams.

So, once you begin to go into prayer, you will also be strengthening your relationship with God. He will begin to show you His heart and He will give you the desires of yours. Psalms 37:4 states, *"Delight yourself also in the Lord, and He shall give you the desires of your heart."*

Come before Him boldly because Jesus Christ has given you access to the Father.

"Ask, and it will be given to you; seek, and you will find; knock, and it will be opened to you. [8] For everyone who asks receives, and he who seeks finds, and to him who knocks it will be opened." Matthew 7:7-8

PRAYER

Father God, I pray that I will be able to experience God dreams and that through the dreams I will be transformed through His messages. Lord, I believe in the scriptures because they are true and I know that if You want to relay a message to me through dreams it will be done. Jesus name I pray. Amen!

What is God telling you?

_____

_____

_____

_____

The Hope

Many times life has a way of knocking the air out of us and leaving us without hope. The antonym of hope is despair and its meaning is the complete loss or absence of hope. But, the scriptures tell us in 2 Corinthians 4:8, *"We are afflicted in every way, but not crushed; perplexed, but not driven to despair;"* (ESV).

Paul is saying that no matter what may come your way do not lose hope. God is our present hope and His desire is to pull you out of despair. If you decide to remain in a state of despair, it would be as if you were turning your back on Hope. Your eyes should not be placed on your present circumstances as though there is no solution to it.

Your hope should remain in the Promises of God over your life and for your family. Faith is a key component while you wait on your solutions, that's when you are keeping hope alive. Hope is a gift of God and one of the *"three things [that] will last forever"* 1 Corinthians 13:13 (NLT).

"Why are you cast down, O my soul, and why are you in turmoil within me? Hope in God; for I shall again praise him, my salvation and my God." **Psalms 43:5 (ESV)**

PRAYER

Lord Jesus, I pray that my hope does not diminish in the midst of my trails and that I may focus my eyes on You. I believe Your promises for my life will come to pass. In the meantime, I will continue to hope.

What is God telling you?

_____

_____

_____

_____

About the Author

Migdalia Centeno is the Founder/President of the Professional Women in Leadership (PWL). She has obtained two Masters' degree in Organizational Leadership and in Human Services. She has been a Licensed Alcohol and Drug Counselor.

She is currently the director of a family counseling program, CURA, Inc., where she has worked for the past 25 years. The program specializes in substance abuse treatment. Becoming a Personal Leadership Coach has been part of her most recent accomplishments.

Migdalia is a Licensed Minister through the Assemblies of God. She has served as an Educator and Director in Sunday School, as a Youth Pastor, Young Couples Pastor, and member of the Deacon Board at her local church. For the past 13 years, she has been a Professor at the Hammonton Assemblies of God Bible Institute in NJ and the Director and Professor of the Spanish Eastern School of Theology (SEST) in the last five years.

Her ministry has consisted of conducting conferences and trainings to groups of all ages which focus on inner healing, deliverance and leadership development. As a conference speaker, she has traveled internationally.

Migdalia married the love of her life and high school sweetheart, Domiason Centeno. He has served as a motivator, encourager, and supporter. He has empowered her to pursue the highest potential in her education and leadership. Through their marriage of 35 years, God has blessed them with the honor of having two wonderful children, Millicent and Dommasin who are also active in their ministry.

Author's Notes

Pivotal moments in my life:

"I cannot do it on my own, I need you Jesus!"

"The Holy Spirit breathed life into my soul."

"I was unable to speak, and all I could do was cry."

"I allowed myself to be a victim of self-pity."

"I no longer felt empty."

"I wanted to praise God, but I felt unworthy…"

"I was designed to spiritually prosper and endure life's trails."

"Henceforth, the evidence of the believer's fruits will be visible."

"… I felt nervous and anxious."

"I needed to wait on God…"

"…If I can only touch the hem of His garment, I will be healed…"

"God's will for the believers is to create His identity in their lives…"

"…I said to myself, "What am I doing here?"

"Without noticing, I became a people- pleaser."

"I cannot do it on my own, I need you Jesus!"

"Latina women were not encouraged to further their education."

"I could sense an overwhelming love that was flowing out of Him."

"I was witnessing something that was literally out of this world."

"…I knew that I had to call out to Jesus."

"No one has been able to love me the way Jesus has

loved me."

"I have continued to receive healing…"

"Jesus continues to be available right now."

"I always knew that my hope would be in Jesus…"

"I had to learn how to trust."

"I had Jesus in my heart and He filled me with His

Love."

"God closed Hannah's womb?"

The Power of Forgiveness

Jessica Kastner writes about the Five Truths about the Power of Forgiveness,

> Forgiveness is a staple of the Christian faith. We know that Christ died so we can receive forgiveness, and we know we're called to forgive others. But sometimes we might not fully grasp the necessity and power of true forgiveness due to a lack of knowledge, or feelings of bitterness we haven't dealt with. Here are a few truths to remember about forgiving.

Five Truths about the power of forgiveness:

1. God forgave our sin…even the really bad ones.

2. We might as well forgive, because the offenses will never stop.

3. Vengeance is His.

4. We have to forgive ourselves.

5. Forgiveness leads to freedom.

Jesus forgave the very men nailing him to the cross, and I think there's a reason that detail remained in God's Word. He knows the damage unforgiveness can bring, and he wants the world to see his power and mercy when we do let go, and forgive.

The Salvation Prayer

The Sinner's Prayer (by Dr. Ray Pritchard)

Lord Jesus, for too long I've kept you out of my life. I know that I am a sinner and that I cannot save myself. No longer will I close the door when I hear you knocking. By faith I gratefully receive your gift of salvation. I am ready to trust you as my Lord and Savior. Thank you, Lord Jesus, for coming to earth. I believe you are the Son of God who died on the cross for my sins and rose from the dead on the third day. Thank you for bearing my sins and giving me the gift of eternal life. I believe your words are true. Come into my heart, Lord Jesus, and be my Savior. Amen.

If you have prayed this prayer in sincere faith, you may want to put your initials by the prayer along with today's date as a reminder that you have come to Christ in faith, trusting him as your Lord and Savior.

Resources

https://www.biblegateway.com

https://www.crosswalk.com/faith/prayer/prayers/the-sinners-prayer-4-examples.html

https://www.family.org.sg/fotfs/Articles/Parenting/The_5_A_s_for_Your_Family.aspx

http://diverseeducation.com/article/7827/

http://pastorrick.com/devotional/english/your-heart-is-designed-for-god-to-fill

https://www.desiringgod.org/articles/god-s-grace-is-mind-blowing

https://www.goodreads.com/work/quotes/42756574-pray-like-a-gourmet-creative-ways-to-feed-your-soul

http://davidwilkersontoday.blogspot.com/2017/08/wait-on-holy-spirit-gary-wilkerson.html

Love has a Name…JESUS

https://www.brainyquote.com/quotes/rick_warren_599792

http://www.azquotes.com/quote/712438

http://www.patheos.com/blogs/christiancrier/2014/05/02/what-is-agape-love-a-bible-study/

https://www.thoughtco.com/build-your-relationship-with-jesus-701524

https://www.brainyquote.com/quotes/uma_thurman_481200

https://bible.org/seriespage/lesson-17-stephen-man-acts-68-15

https://www.crosswalk.com/faith/spiritual-life/inspiring-quotes/25-quotes-to-give-you-hope.html

http://www.tdjakes.com/posts/5-t-d-jakes-quotes-about-our-personal-transformation

https://www.ibelieve.com/faith/3-life-changing-truths-to-know-about-encounters-with-god.html

Love has a Name…JESUS

https://www.brainyquote.com/quotes/billy_graham_446521

http://www1.cbn.com/700club/dream-interpretation-according-bible

Bible Versions

English Standard Version (ESV)

New American Standard Bible (NASB)

New King James Version (NKJV)

New Living Translation (NLT)

PERSONAL NOTES

PERSONAL NOTES

Love has a Name…JESUS

Contact Information

Facebook: Dom-Migdalia Centeno

Twitter: Migdalia Centeno

Instagram: Migdalia Centeno

Email Address: Dommigdalia@gmail.com

Migdalia Centeno

Program Development
Personal Leadership Coach
Conference Speaker
Educator/Trainer
Mentorship

27033985R00076

Made in the USA
Columbia, SC
22 September 2018